The Centre for Ente   ...a ˜

            Eth

Quaker Capitalism

Lessons for today

Richard Turnbull

Printed in the United Kingdom

First Printing, 2014

ISBN 1-910666-00-5

Published by:
Centre for Enterprise, Markets and Ethics
31 Beaumont Street
Oxford OX1 2NP

Contents

1 Setting the scene

The aim of this publication is to explore why the Quakers were so prominent in business, the reasons for their success, and to consider what lessons we can learn for today.

The Industrial Revolution was a cauldron of invention, innovation and creativity. This economic activity led to extraordinary economic growth in the period 1770–1870. Output per capita doubled between 1760 and 1830; industrial investment – measured by gross domestic fixed capital formation – rose per annum from under £1 million in the 1760s to £5 million by the 1810s to over £13 million by the 1840s.[1] There were vast movements of population from country to city, and new industries grew up, especially in manufacturing, both of which factors brought new challenges for society. The dispersed poverty and low incomes that had characterised rural, agrarian England became concentrated in the new urban conurbations. Economic challenges also emerged, exemplified in the debate around the Corn Laws – which imposed tariffs on imported grain and so ensured that the price of bread was kept high in the domestic market, to the benefit of the producer and detriment of the consumer. The triumph of cheap bread on a large scale over agricultural incomes was a portrait of the age; rural England was no longer dominant. This was also the age of capital – its generation, accumulation and investment. The relationship between capital, production, labour and society occupied an important place in national debate.

The fact that religious people took an interest in these matters, especially those of poverty and social welfare, is unsurprising.

That a small, intricate, rather idiosyncratic group – the Quakers – lay at the heart not simply of the response to poverty but of the innovation and creation of new industries, is little known, and perhaps, at least on the surface, rather more surprising.

To this group of religious adherents we owe a great deal in the development of both banking and manufacturing industry. John Freame (1669–1745), who established a partnership in Lombard Street in 1690 that today we know as Barclays, was a Quaker. Another Quaker, Samuel Lloyd, like his father, in the iron trade, together with a Unitarian, John Taylor, established Taylors and Lloyds – later Lloyds Bank – in Birmingham in 1765. Joseph Pease (1799–1872) came from a prominent Quaker family in the north east of England with interests in railways, mining and manufacturing as well as banking. He was the first Quaker able to take his seat in Parliament. The exclusion of the Quakers from public life (further explained in section 2.2) is one reason why, politically, they tended to support the Whigs (the more progressive or liberal of the two parties at the time) and developed a wide social vision. The Pease family were prominent in the promotion of the Stockton and Darlington Railway Company – the world's first public railway to use steam locomotives. Another Quaker banking family, the Gurneys, later part of Barclays, also contributed to the capital. Quaker banking finance underpinned a good deal of industrial expansion.

The Quakers, like most religious groups, were committed to the care and welfare of those within their community. The close-knit nature of the Quakers, this sense of responsibility, together with an acute business judgement, enabled them to see the need for 'life assurance'. They saw this as prudent provision rather than 'second guessing' God. The fact that Quakers, due to their self-disciplined lives, lived longer than average, illustrated this business wisdom and was rather helpful for the business model of a life-assurance society. So it was that 45 Quakers, in early 1832, subscribed £10,700 of initial capital for a life fund. What began as Friends Provident and became Friends Life now has £120 billion of funds under management and remains organised as a mutual.

Among the many memorial stones in the Quaker graveyard above Coalbrookdale in Shropshire lies that of Abraham Darby (1678–1717) – the founder of a great dynasty of ironmasters, an industry in which the Quakers were prominent in several ways.

> A scrutiny of the iron trade during the
> eighteenth century soon reveals that the
> Quakers were a very prominent element in
> the structure of the industry, and were
> contributing heavily, not only by the
> provision of capital, but by technical
> improvements, to the trade's advancement.[2]

After an apprenticeship Darby established a foundry in
Bristol for the manufacture of domestic pots and pans –
more palatable than canon and munitions. In 1708 he
took over a derelict foundry in Coalbrookdale. Through
technological advances, together with both horizontal
(buying other foundries) and vertical (securing the
sources of the raw materials) integration, Darby and his
son, also Abraham, transformed a local, unused forge
into nothing less than the laboratory for the industrial
revolution.

The best known Quaker manufacturer is probably the
Cadbury family of Birmingham. Even today the picture
of the cricket pitch in front of the factory is a reminder
of the original, inclusive vision for business. Joseph Fry
from 1748, John Cadbury from 1824, Henry and then
Joseph Rowntree from 1862 were business people from
Quaker families who established and developed the
manufacture of chocolate. Their vision saw the business
as an extension of the family and hence the
responsibilities of family extended to the workforce. This
vision also extended beyond the factories, not least in the

case of John Cadbury's sons, George and Richard, with the development of the Bournville model village (we will return to the model villages in section 3.3).

The extent of Quaker involvement in manufacturing and banking is startling. Not only iron forges, chocolate, banking and life assurance, but also shoe-making (C. & J. Clark of Street), biscuits (Huntley & Palmer of Reading), pharmaceuticals (Allen & Hanburys of Bethnal Green), soap and chemicals (Joseph Crosfield & Sons) – only to mention a selection.

The picture we can draw is fascinating but also complex. Not all Quakers established businesses, and of those that did not all succeeded or became household names. The close-knit nature of the Quaker communities (or, to be rather more blunt, their control over their members) meant that the penalties for failure – especially bankruptcy – could be severe, usually resulting in expulsion.

Realities also changed over time with the challenges of integrating business, family and faith. As we will see, some successful business Quakers left the faith, others abandoned some of the distinctive Quaker characteristics such as plain dress – and some faithfully continued to follow their beliefs and to seek to follow its principles in business and in the use of their wealth.

The population of Britain in 1850 was around 27 million. The Quakers, as a group, were already declining in number, and amounted to some 15,000 people, a little over a half of one percent of the population. There remains something fascinating about the disproportionate presence of Quakers in the development of our finance and industry. Equally captivating is the realisation that from this group of religious pioneers there are lessons today for industry, commerce, economy and society.

2   Why were the Quakers successful in business?

To appreciate the reasons why the Quakers we successful in business we need, first of all, to understand who they were and what factors formed and shaped them.

2.1   The origins of the Quakers

The Quakers as a group derived from the ministry of George Fox (1624–91). They emerged at the time of another revolution, the last bloody event on English soil, the Civil Wars of 1642–49. From the restoration of Charles II in 1660 through to yet another revolution, this time the bloodless 'glorious revolution' of 1688 – when William of Orange and his wife, Mary, were invited from the Netherlands to take the English throne jointly, in place of James II, forced into exile, his Catholicism unacceptable – and the slow dawn of a more tolerant age, the Quakers were formed and shaped in a period of some of the most intense religious persecution since the reign of Mary Tudor (1553–58). This had a profound impact on their preparation for industry. Quakers suffered immensely in the persecutions of non-Anglicans – such as Jews, Catholics and non-conformists – that mars both Christian and English history. Their spirituality was sincere, based on the external guidance of the Scripture and the inner guidance of the Spirit ('the inner light').

They met together, supported each other, held each other to account and considered themselves accountable to God for their lives – including the conduct of business.

The Quakers were an expression of dissent with a strong emphasis on freedom, including from the state and from the established Church. George Fox sought to establish neither a denomination nor even a spiritual movement. However, the Quakers represented a spiritual vitality that the governments in turn of Charles I, Oliver Cromwell and Charles II found difficult to contain. Fox's spiritual home originated with the classic Puritans, Calvinists who sought to build Geneva in England (that is, English followers of John Calvin who wished to replicate his doctrines and practices). This was a rather austere form of institutional religion that certainly inculcated hard work – the Protestant work ethic – and a rugged individualism but, at least for some, left the heart cold. Fox soon left this behind in the quest for spiritual experience, the direct speaking of God and powerful experiential preaching. The term 'Quaker' was used originally in the sense of 'trembling before the Lord' and was adopted by both adherents and opponents.

At the heart of Quaker convictions was the idea of the inner light. This powerful, life-changing force was present in all people, and it was the Spirit that guided the believer into the true interpretation of Scripture. As with classic Puritanism, this light showed up sin, but for the Quaker it was also the light of Christ that was 'the active principle of God within us, working for our salvation'.

> The doctrine of the light was a doctrine of
> the real presence of Christ as fundamental to
> the Friends as transubstantiation to the post-
> Tridentine Roman Catholics, and capable of
> generating the same power and conviction.[3]

So from around 1652 the Quakers began to organise. The message was receiving a ready hearing, not least in rural areas. The like-minded began to meet and, lacking clergy or buildings, the worship varied from a silent waiting upon the Spirit to more vocal and formal acts of worship.

Cromwell's 'Commonwealth' lasted from the execution of Charles I in 1649 to his death in 1658. This was the period of English history when no King reigned; at least not in name. He was succeeded by his son, Richard, who was not a success and was forced from office in less than a year. Tired of the austerity, religious and otherwise, demands were made for the restoration of the monarchy – Charles' son returned from exile to take the throne as Charles II. Radical religion was seen as a challenge to order and was not tolerated. Around 2,000 ministers were forced from their posts. The viciousness of the Clarendon Code, the series of repressive measures enacted by Edward Hyde, the Earl of Clarendon, in the restoration government of Charles II, was almost a last gasp of religious oppression in England, at least of the more explicit sort. The measures were aimed at all varieties of the Puritans, who had underpinned the previous republican government. The Corporation Act (1661) required all holders of public office to take Holy Communion according to the rites of the Church of England and to reject Cromwell's Commonwealth. The Act of Uniformity (1662) imposed the Book of Common Prayer. The Conventicle Act (1664) prevented more than five people meeting together for worship unless belonging to the same household, and the Five Mile Act (1665) forbade ministers who had left their livings – being unable to swear the necessary oaths under the Act of Uniformity – from coming within five miles of their previous churches or residences. Many suffered under these unjust provisions. The Quakers, radical dissenters both spiritually and politically, were among the most persecuted.

The early Quakers were neither the poorest in society nor drawn from the ranks of the gentry. [4] They were thus rather 'the middling sort', the emerging middle class. Skilled artisans and modest merchants were drawn to the quietness of the Quaker meeting, the intimacy of fellowship and an experience of religion designed to equip them for daily life. A rather intricate structure developed, though one which served Quaker culture and control rather well. As well as the weekly meeting for worship, there was also, for administrative purposes, a Monthly Meeting (either a single congregation or several in a local area), a Quarterly Meeting (regional) and the powerful

London Yearly Meeting (national). Excluded from civic and political society under the oppressive measures of the Earl of Clarendon (as well as exclusion from local or national political office Quakers and other dissenters could not enter the universities), many of these families turned their attention to business and enterprise; and with remarkable tenacity and not inconsiderable – though not universal – success. Perhaps it was the innate creativity of the artisan combined with a serious and meaningful spirituality that gave the Quakers that motivation to succeed. Persecution hardened the resolve. Yet, despite many problems, they understood some basic principles, including integrity, trust, the importance of confidence in financial dealings, discipline and responsibility. This responsibility extended to both employees and to the wider society in which business was set. These characteristics may not have been exclusively 'Quaker' but the Quaker experience of exclusion meant that they gave even greater weight to these aspects of practical dealings with each other and also, as a sign of witness, with others. Work assumed spiritual importance (both God and other Quakers needed to see this hard work), and as a spiritual tradition without clergy, the actions of each individual assumed more significance in the public square. The Quaker had to be seen acting properly.

2.2   Quaker culture

Some scholars see the link of culture and entrepreneurship as the determinative factor in what they describe as 'the Quaker success story'.[5] That there is such a link is now widely accepted. So, 'the quality of entrepreneurship depends upon the quality of business culture',[6] which in turn is built upon trust, thus reducing transaction costs, as does co-operation between family firms and indeed the existence of external networks. These are crucial factors in understanding the Quaker business story.

> The membership of the Society of Friends, however, was instilled with a high moral culture, the product in part of an extensive family and kinship network. This, together with an inherited religious code emphasising spiritual priorities, redounded to the advantage of Quaker men of business in terms of confidence and expectations.[7]

The basic building block of this Quaker culture was the experience of spiritually minded merchants facing exclusion and persecution turning their skill and passion to business. There is good evidence that merchants, artisans and craftsmen were overrepresented in those attracted to the Quakers. Indeed the proportion of Quakers involved in industry and commerce may have been as much as 5–10 times the proportion of the general population so involved.[8] This rather supports the earlier observation that Quakerism appealed more to the middle classes than either gentry or labourer. These figures derive from the earliest period of the Quaker expansion in the latter part of the seventeenth century. However, if the Quaker faith was established among these groups, it is less surprising that at the dawn of the industrial revolution 100 years later these families were at the forefront.

The added factor to the 'natural disposition' of those families that were attracted to Quakerism was the impact of the 150 years of exclusion and persecution. Nothing was more likely to hone the entrepreneurial spirit than the attempt to extinguish it. The early Quakers attracted the suspicion of disloyalty. Interrupting sermons in the parish church may not have helped their cause, but there was a healthy scepticism towards the establishment – whether the ruler was Charles I, Oliver Cromwell or Charles II. Under the Clarendon Code the Quakers suffered both direct persecution (imprisonment) and indirect (exclusion from universities, from civic life and from certain professions). The Corporation Act effectively excluded them from both civic and professional life in the 'corporate' cities – that is, those established under a charter. This explains some of the regional variations in Quaker strength. A merchant, trader or craftsman facing what effectively amounts to restraint of trade in a large city will leave and live somewhere where trade is possible. The constraints ranged from fines for non-attendance at Anglican worship through to the inability to sue for the recovery of debt. The largest city in England that did not operate under a charter of incorporation was Birmingham, and so this city became a centre for Quaker entrepreneurial activity. Indeed this heritage of a free and tolerant city meant that Birmingham became the centre for a more liberal social vision of society through the later reforming work of Joseph Chamberlain and the Whigs, supported by, but going beyond, Quakerism itself. Birmingham also became the location of the Quaker model village of Bournville – to which we will return.

A further cultural factor that affected Quaker entrepreneurship was exclusion not only from civic life but also from universities. This led to the Quakers valuing education all the more, founding their own schools and providing business education within the community through the development of apprenticeships.

> Minds which in the universities would have provided the research workers and scholars, were diverted into business, and found their most congenial outlet in the more technical businesses, where an aptitude for study could find expression in experiment and observation.[9]

This may go some way to explaining why the Darbys and others flourished in the iron industry, not only in trading but also in technical development. The Darbys might have been expected to attend University but they could not do so. Perhaps it also explains the quest within Cadburys for the ideal recipe for chocolate.

The first Quaker school was established in 1668 by George Fox himself and by 1671 there were 15 such educational institutions. There was further expansion as direct – but not indirect – persecution eased with the passage of the Toleration Act of 1689. The cultural impact of persecution, however, led Quakers to seek Quaker teachers and imposed Quaker discipline in Quaker schools. Certain subjects – music and dance, for example, lay outside the acceptable bounds of Quaker culture, but the consequence was that more attention was paid to practical subjects, ranging from construction to agriculture.

In the run-up to the industrial transformation of England in the late eighteenth and early nineteenth centuries, Quaker culture had been successfully transmitted into the new age. The Quaker school was a key means of this transmission. Ironically, as persecution eased, Quaker numbers declined. Education, however, became ever more important. Dr John Fothergill, a prominent Quaker born in 1714, was concerned that the existing Quaker schools were struggling. Together with David Barclay and the York tea merchant William Tuke, the necessary funds were raised and plans laid for a new fee-paying Quaker school at Ackworth. The school was in essence an extended Quaker family. This was precisely how many Quakers would subsequently run their businesses. Among the many functions exercised by Ackworth and other Quaker schools was ensuring that 'its pupils would remain Quakers'.[10] It did so by consolidating family ties, providing opportunities for marriage and in preparation for life as a Quaker. Ackworth officially opened in 1779. In 1816 John Joseph Gurney, the prominent Quaker banker, worried about the lack of scriptural knowledge at the school made provision for each pupil to receive a Bible upon arrival, rather than as a leaving gift. This simple act was a symptom of a problem that faced the Quakers: was their dependence on Scripture or the inner light? The Quaker moral code was dependent, for many, on the objective teaching of Scripture. However, the wider vision for society often drew upon that inner light of conscience. The Quakers were not exempt from theological disputes.

Ackworth became a regional centre of importance for the Quaker movement. The links to the Quaker involvement in industry are amply demonstrated by the foundation of Friends Provident in 1831. Two former scholars of the school, Samuel Tuke and Joseph Rowntree, were particularly concerned about the consequences for the wife and family of a young teacher there, Henry Brady, who died in 1828 at the age of 30. Responsibility for caring for the family fell upon the Quaker 'Monthly Meeting'. The two businessmen demonstrated a fascinating insight into how to bring commercial practice to bear in the solution of social problems. The 1831 annual gathering of Friends at the school agreed to establish a life assurance society for the benefit of Friends. In the first instance the classes of business to be written were annuities, endowment life policies and children's deferred policies. The initial capital was subscribed in 1832 by 45 prominent Quakers at 5 per cent. The promoters saw their plans as appropriate provision for families rather than any distrust in God, and were quite open about the commercial benefit of longer than average life expectancy among the Friends. Suggestions that the idea of life assurance amounted to a 'lottery', speculation or gambling were rejected; such ideas were anathema to the Friends. The initial memorandum summarised the position well:

> [the Institution] is not a charitable association, but it simply enables those who unite in it to help themselves.[11]

A further impact of exclusion was the increase in the provision of apprenticeships within the Quaker community, often financed through the wills of Quaker families. The Quakers came closer together through the impact of persecution, and apprenticeships within the community were one way of ensuring continued community cohesion and indeed the passing on of Quaker culture and values. Apprenticeship thus served the dual function of preparation for a trade and the preserving of cultural identity. So Abraham Darby was apprenticed to a Birmingham Quaker, married within the Friends and became a partner in a Bristol metal company before moving to Coalbrookdale. Joseph Crosfield was apprenticed to a Quaker chemist prior to establishing his own soap-making business. Apprenticeship was, of course, a normal route into industry at the time. George Fox had emphasised the importance of apprenticeships and provided for the necessary oversight of the 'Monthly Meetings' and indeed for their financial provision. Many Quaker businesses were family concerns and these also provided ready routes into the business for family members – for example, the Pease family with its extensive interests in wool, weaving and banking as well as mining and railways.

Good business practice, innovation, entrepreneurship and a passion for education and training – not least given the exclusion from the universities – all contributed to Quaker entry into business. All of these characteristics were encouraged by the Quaker experience. Similarly, these practices and experiences together formed and shaped the Quaker culture that provided the context and setting for the business enterprise. A strong culture is central to business success. An inquisitive and creative mind is crucial for both entrepreneurial and technological success. The Quakers provided both. Only as the Quaker culture weakened did many Quaker business families begin to move away from Quaker principles.

2.3   Quaker spirituality

Purpose determines behaviour and action. The consequences of current patterns of behaviour influence deeply the business and corporate context of future generations. In other words, the custodians and practitioners of contemporary businesses have a responsibility to shape not only the present but the future. The history of the business corporation has been one of the gradual separation of ownership and control, exemplified by the development of both the joint-stock company and the concept of limited liability. Thus the company took on a separate legal identity. This raised several problems. Can a company have a moral purpose? How is the legal personality of the company to ensure that the long-term best interests of future generations are protected?

> The amoral nature of the corporation and the failure to internalize the well-being of future generations are intrinsically interrelated.[12]

The idea of stewardship links purpose with responsibility for the future. Indeed this is one reason why the family business has been such an important form of business organisation. The idea of family encapsulates both purpose and stewardship for the future. There is both an interest in preserving a vision within a family and a ready means of succession. Religion is also concerned with the stewardship of the present for the benefit of the future, whether in terms of individual destiny, the family or business practice. Religion will often be the catalyst for the development of codes of behaviour and ethics. The success of the Quakers in business derived at least to some extent from their clear code of moral behaviour together with a vision for the future of the family firm and indeed of wider society.

Spirituality was central to their success. Spirituality is concerned with the nature of the individual's relationship with God rather than the system of doctrinal and dogmatic beliefs that may characterise a particular faith. Indeed for Quakers an experiential spirituality was their distinctive characteristic. The 'inner light' or conscience determined their behaviour, although external Scriptures also provided a guide; indeed there was some tension between the two. Quaker theology was not static. However, there are a number of good reasons why the Quaker spirituality shaped their business practice.

Spirituality and business practice

First, the spirituality of the Quakers developed character. So George Cadbury wrote that the

> . . . training of Friends . . . gave them qualities
> most likely to lead to success in business.
> They were taught self-denial, rigid abstinence
> from all luxury and self-indulgence.[13]

These characteristics were of particular importance for an entrepreneur. The business of entrepreneurship involved not only innovation and risk-taking but also a clear vision, a well-shaped purpose and patience. Success was often a long time in the waiting. The characteristically Quaker discipline of life and mind was ideal preparation for the wait for economic return. Frugality only enhanced the prospects of success and also increased the sense of responsibility that came with wealth.

Second, the Quaker conviction of the 'light within' gave them clarity, commitment and compassion. This gave the Friends an inner focus – God had called them – and, with the belief that this light shone, at least to some extent, in all people, a vision for respect and flourishing of others. This inner light also gave them a vision for society. The problem with the idea of 'inner light' was subjectivity. In their quest for consensus the Quakers turned not to Scriptures, creeds or councils but to 'quietism' – waiting upon God for guidance. In later years these Quakers looked to Robert Barclay (1648–90) and his theological exposition of the 'light within', which was effectively the sole guarantee against creeds, councils and denominations – the cause of so much historic suffering for the Quakers. The light within the heart of every person was the essence of truth. This certainly gave Quakers inner conviction and marked them out from many others. Although this may go some way to explain Quaker compassion and conviction, conscience alone is unlikely to be sufficient for business ethics. Here the distinctively Quaker contribution is formed by the experience of conscience being combined with authoritative revelation.

Hence the third element was the characteristic evangelical[14] emphasis on Scripture. This may seem unusual when Quakers are so often seen as resistant to external authorities. However, adherence to a clear doctrine of Scripture was characteristic of aspects of Quakerism from the beginning and dominant in much of late eighteenth- and early nineteenth-century Quakerism, not least among prominent business Quakers such as Joseph John Gurney. It was this 'evangelical Quakerism' that transformed the inner light of conscience into objective standards of moral behaviour and gave the Quakers an explicit moral code. If the Quaker mentality had been shaped only by the conviction of inner light then morality would have remained essentially subjective. The heightened sense of both sin and righteous behaviour that evangelicalism supplied was an essential underpinning of the Quaker moral code for business. The longer-term decline of this aspect of Quakerism may also explain, at least in part, something of the decline of its business ethic. In other words, as the Quakers lost something of the objectivity of the Scriptures as a guiding force (hard ethics), behaviour became more determined by subjective conscience (soft ethics). The key to an effective business ethic lies in the application of both hard and soft ethical approaches.

There was clearly some tension between 'inner light' and external authority. The 'Yearly Meeting' of 1829 asserted the authority of Scripture, and Gurney, the Norwich banker, had clear reservations on the doctrine of the inner light. However, alongside scriptural authority,

Gurney asserted not the classic Puritan notion of predestination – that is, that all things, including eternal destiny, were predetermined – but that all humanity had received an element of the divine spark: 'in the midst of his ruin by the fall, he is visited with a ray of heavenly light independently of any outward revelation.'[15] The prevalence of sin in a fallen world demanded right conduct. However, the universality of the divine spark encouraged both individual compassion and social vision. This was a further example of how the Quakers adapted to changing context. Puritan faith, however doctrinally orthodox, could seem dry and rationalistic. John Wesley, in his part in the eighteenth-century awakening known as the Evangelical Revival, gave weight to the experiential alongside the doctrinal. Indeed this experiential shift in evangelicalism may have contributed to Quaker decline. Wesley opposed much of Quaker doctrine (and radicalism), yet personal experience of God lay as much at the heart of the Wesleyan revival as it did with the Quakers.

So from the point of view of the Quaker in business, the essential moral code for life and work in a fallen world derived from both the revealed norms in Scripture and an experiential appropriation of that code to real life; neither simply conscience nor rule-bound, but a dynamic appropriation of both.

2.4 Quaker morality

This dynamic transformed early Quaker business practice.

> . . . their refusal to separate business activities from the principles and disciplines which regulated their religious life, gave them a stability and soundness of practice that was unusual in their day.[16]

And, so it would seem, also in our day – all too often business life and personal ethics (not to mention any religious convictions) seem to be compartmentalised.

George Fox and subsequently the 'Yearly Meetings' were particularly concerned to ensure the appropriate regulation of Quaker conduct because of the link in such a close-knit community between conduct, distinctiveness and identity. The prevalence of Quakers in business – with all of the moral peril that entailed – meant that explicit guidance on business practice was likely to feature with some significance. This guidance was given through 'Advices' and 'Queries' issued at first by Fox himself and then through the well-organised network of meetings. The content of these advices and queries is highly instructive.

Right behaviour in business certainly meant avoiding bankruptcy. The Quakers had a highly structured system of oversight of their members. Bankruptcy was possibly the worst sin that could be committed as it would bring the Friends into disrepute. Hence the 'Monthly' and 'Yearly Meetings' were very interested in the business activities of the Friends and were not short on offering advice.

Hence, it is not surprising, though certainly instructive, that an early advice on trade in 1675 warned Quakers not to trade beyond their means and to keep their word in all things. To put it another way, they were advised to practise prudence and honesty. In 1692 they were advised not to delay the payment of just debts and to be cautious about running up debt themselves. How many small and medium enterprises today report on the weight of extended credit terms taken by customers they supply? As an oppressed minority or at least as a group suffering under legal disability, reputation for honesty and integrity in trade dealings became integral to Quaker identity.

Extraordinarily, at least in the light of contemporary experience, an advice of 1732 exhorts Friends to be 'careful not to involve themselves in business which they understand not' – a salutary warning for all boards today. Issues of governance and board responsibility are not new; indeed the quality of board oversight is central to virtuous behaviour. In 1793 an advice called on Friends to ensure that they kept clear and accurate accounts, which should be inspected once a year – a provision predating the Companies Act! Solvency, accuracy, honest and trust were central to the Quaker moral code.

> It was this unshakeable honesty of the
> Quaker that made people willing to place
> their money in his hands when most other
> people were suspect, and which opened the
> way for the success of the Quaker bankers.[17]

Honesty extended to pricing and weights and measures. The importance of this in the context of the times is that weights and measures were areas of significant commercial abuse. Commerce and trade was, all too often, conducted between unequal partners in which the relationship of power was often the final determinant of price. In the seventeenth century and onwards it was usual to haggle over the price of everything. This was as much the case in business-to-business dealings as it was in direct retail situations with customers. However, for many ordinary folk this led to great uncertainty as well as the danger of unequal or unfair dealings. The Quaker emphasis on truth led them to be pioneers of fixed pricing. So people again began to place their trust in the Quaker merchants – they could rely on both the quality of goods to be supplied and the guarantee and honesty of a fixed-price transaction.

2.5   Quaker networks

The Quakers knew each other. They also did business with each other. As a relatively small group, bound together very closely by both the experience of persecution and the resulting cultural identity, their network transcended both geography and family. This network provided hospitality, support, trade routes, capital flows and marriages.

> Quaker homes could be a forum for discussing mutual commercial interests, where business advice was proffered and accepted, where deals were struck and opportunities pursued.[18]

As previously noted the Society of Friends was structured around a system of meetings, 'Monthly Meetings,' 'Quarterly Meetings,' and the London 'Yearly Meeting.' The prominence of significant Quaker families at each level reinforced the interconnectedness of the Society. These connections also allowed Quakers not only to conduct business with each other but also to be a highly effective channel for commercial information. Details were shared about experience in trading, markets, participants – who not to trade with! – and so on. The Quaker networks were not only national but also international – allowing the savvy Quaker trader to exploit in particular the large American market. One example given by James Walvin in *The Quakers: Money and Morals* is that of the apothecary Thomas Corbyn who, trading not only across the English provinces but also through the Quaker networks, broke into both American and West Indian markets. Trust was invaluable in international trade. This point is reinforced when considering the English market. Indeed some scholars argue that it may have been the network system more than the religious ethic that was the reason for business success.

> . . . the picture of a religious ethic acting directly upon the individual oversimplifies the direct impact of ideas upon events, by ignoring the opportunities and strength given by the fact of community amongst the faithful . . . The world of religious-cum-kinship group provided an environment of mutual trust and confidence within which a private 'invisible hand' could accommodate the advantages of each member with the benefit of all.[19]

A similar point is made in George Sutton's history of the Somerset shoemakers C. & J. Clark. In essence Sutton argues that the success of James and Cyrus owed nothing to religious conviction: they displayed the same characteristics as all successful entrepreneurs, but when it came to the need for capital the Quaker network came into its own. Hence the 'Quaker formula for success was therefore, in C. & J. Clark's case, group responsibility and action' and that it 'was Quaker unity, not the uniquely Quaker qualities possessed by the Clark family's individual members, which accounted for the C. & J. Clark's continued existence in 1863'.[20]

Commentators righty draw attention to the power of the Quaker network. In doing so, however, they potentially lose something of the impact of the religious convictions themselves. Both George Sutton and Deborah Cadbury, in their histories of Clarks and Cadburys, mention the suspicion of the firms towards advertising – which at least suggests that something of their convictions were brought to bear. The Quaker networks were undoubtedly important, but to overemphasise these at the expense of convictions elevates a sociological analysis above that of ideas. Quaker businesses certainly faced moral dilemmas, but convictions were important: the Darby iron-making interests diverted their energies to the domestic market rather than the traditional military one; the Gurney bank refused to accept subscriptions from privateers in the 1770s. The decision about business and with whom to conduct it was a moral one over which the Quaker businesses exercised careful judgement.

Perhaps one of the most significant features of the Quaker networks was that they allowed for an efficient and effective flow of capital – essentially they acted as an early capital market. Indeed the Gracechurch Street Meeting – the City of London Quaker meeting – not only attracted some of the wealthiest merchants in London but included many of the Quaker banking families; it was an extraordinarily effective credit reference agency.[21]

A vivid example of the role of the network in providing capital is shown by the involvement of the Quaker banking network in the financing of the Stockton and Darlington Railway. This line holds a fascinating place in the memory of English industrial history as the first public railway in England; it was opened in 1825. What is less well known about is the involvement of the Quaker networks. The Quaker bankers, perhaps attuned to the idea of 'trade routes' facilitated by the Quaker networks, were involved in financing a number of significant transport infrastructure projects – canals, bridges and railways. The particular issue of railways was that the capital requirements were usually beyond those of traditional families or partnerships. So it was that the Pease family of County Durham established interests in the woollen trade. Edward Pease (1711–85) expanded into banking, which was further developed by his son Joseph (1737–1808). Joseph's son, another Edward (1767–1858), was a rather austere Quaker with a scepticism of wealth. The Pease family was also involved in mining, and it was Edward, notwithstanding his plain Quaker dress and spiritual preoccupations, who realised the need for better transport links – a project that began with a canal and ended up with the Stockton and Darlington Railway. The initial subscription was raised in 1818 but there were several hurdles of both politics and economics to overcome. In the case of the latter it was the need for capital that extended beyond the interests and capabilities of the Pease family. The 'bankers of the cousinhood',[22] stepped in. Two Quaker banks, the

Gurneys of Norwich and the more local Backhouses, subscribed a third of the capital – £120,900.

There are a number of points to note. First, the subscriptions were backed by trust and confidence built through the intermarriage of the Quaker networks. The Gurney banking family of Norwich not only knew of the successful trading enterprises of the Pease family but were related by marriage. Edward Pease's son, also called Joseph (1799–1872), married a member of the Gurney family (Emma, John Joseph Gurney's daughter); he also became the first Quaker MP in 1832, as a Whig. The Gurneys had confidence in placing their money. Second, it was personal wealth rather than bank deposits that was used for the capital investment. Railway finance at this time was both risky and notoriously illiquid. By backing a public subscription with their own wealth the Quaker bankers also demonstrated their own credibility, reliability and confidence. Where the Quakers banking businesses as such came into their own was in the provision of both long-term and short-term finance, trade credit and banking transactions.

Quaker bankers could supply them, and they did so abundantly. A banker demonstrated his safety not only by visible wealth in land and urban property, but also by publicly financing such major public utility projects and bringing other bankers in with him. It was not the capital of banks that ensured their soundness, but the visible wealth and connections of those who owned and ran them.[23]

Indeed that point may help to explain, at least in part, the dilution of Quaker influence in business, namely that it was more personal than corporate.

Scholars seem generally to have concluded that it was the network that shaped the Quaker business enterprise.

The purchase of the Middlesbrough Estate provides further striking evidence of the strength of Quaker financial networks. The existence of such a personalised capital market certainly lends support to the notion that as businessmen Quakers were unusually advantaged. In other words, the critical contribution of Quakerism to economic and industrial development is to be found in its distinctive institutional aspects rather than in its religious precepts.[24]

The importance of the Quaker business network should not be overlooked. The careful, precise and formal nature of Quaker structures contributed to a free-flowing network across families, geography and markets. However, it is simplistic to define Quaker business success only in this way. Their moral integrity drawn from their spiritual convictions formed and shaped within a distinctive culture provided the substance of their success. With minds excluded from universities and a culture already well represented among the merchant community, entrepreneurship and innovation were likely to be central to Quaker existence.

3   The business enterprise as family

The next major area of investigation is the idea of the business as family. Ideas, values and culture were, in turn, protected, transmitted and diluted through families. In addition to that dynamic view of family, the Quakers, though not exclusively, understood the business as an extended family. This had significant implications for the conduct of the internal processes of business – employee relations and responsibilities – but also for the growth and development of business itself.

3.1 The family business and limited liability

The early Quaker businesses were family affairs. This was, of course, the normal type of business organisation in the eighteenth and early nineteenth centuries. Some of these businesses grew into dynasties, household names in which the business was passed down generations.

The early Quaker founders had two characteristics that were transmitted down the family business and might be summarised as faith and culture. The strength of the Christian commitment of the early founders was usually passed down the generations because of the power of Quaker culture. However, this did not always last and both the commitment and culture were diluted over time.

> The characteristics of British business, then,
> in the years before the 1870s were those of
> small, if growing, size, of private ownership,
> and the combination of management and
> ownership by a single family.[25]

The Quaker business families established themselves in manufacturing, banking and insurance. As family companies with a strong culture, it was easier to pass these commitments on. However, as both the challenges of wealth and success grew and the Quakers as a group continued to weaken as generations passed, so the hold of Quaker culture on their family businesses weakened. In addition to that, the need for capital, the introduction of joint-stock companies and, most importantly, of limited liability in 1856 further weakened the cultural and spiritual hold of the Quaker families over the businesses they had founded.

The impact of the dynasties can be shown with some examples. The origins of the Fry-family chocolate empire went back to Joseph Fry (1728–87), who began the manufacturing enterprise in Bristol. So the business passed on through his son, Joseph Storrs Fry (1767–1835), and subsequently his own three sons, Joseph, Francis and Richard, joined the firm. Joseph (1795–1879) became one of the world's leading collectors of Bibles and Testaments. His son, also Joseph Storrs Fry (1826–1913), became the chairman of the family firm in 1913.

The Rowntrees show a similar pattern of passing on the stewardship of the family business. The entry into cocoa and chocolate by Henry Isaac Rowntree (1838–83) in 1862, later joined by his brother Joseph (1836–1925), also brought through marriage three prominent Quaker families – the Rowntrees, the Seebohms and the Tukes – into both familial and business relationships. Joseph's father, also Joseph, was a master grocer, having opened a shop in York in 1822.

The same dynastic tendencies can be seen in the Cadburys. This family too were established Quaker merchants. In 1824 John Cadbury, son of Richard Tapper Cadbury, a Quaker, opened his grocer's shop in Birmingham, moving a few years later into the manufacturing process. His brother, Benjamin, joined him in 1847 and the business continued with his sons, Richard and George, from 1861. George's eldest son, Edward, joined the family business in 1893, retiring in 1943 in the position of chairman.

The Gurneys were an extraordinary Quaker dynasty. The family became known for banking, social concern and philanthropy. They intermarried with another famous Quaker banking family, the Barclays. The family bank was established in 1770 by John and Henry Gurney. Control passed through several generations – including John's nephews Richard Gurney (1742–1811), who married into the Barclays, and John Gurney (1749–1811). John's children included Samuel, Joseph John and Elizabeth – later Elizabeth Fry. Through merger the bank became

Overend Gurney. It collapsed in 1866, ten years after Samuel's death. The Gurneys showed the strength of the Quaker networks, but also that being a Quaker was no guarantee against failure. The problem of Overend Gurney was essentially one of succession. Samuel Gurney and David Chapman had established a highly successful bill broking business; low margin on high turnover. Those that succeeded them took risks. They took on bills that were illiquid and some were fraudulent. The collapsing loan book also reached the family's country bank in Norwich. Bizarrely the partners tried to float the firm, already insolvent, in 1865. Rumour spread, deposits fell and on 10th May 1866 Overend Gurney stopped paying on its bills. The shareholders lost a fortune as did the family which had given guarantees. The directors were prosecuted, unsuccessfully. Although only 2 of the 6 directors were still Quakers, and the cousinhood were greatly relieved, the damage in terms of confidence and trust was immense.

The problems faced by a family business of the eighteenth and nineteenth centuries were not, in essence, different from today – how to ensure effective succession and issues around the raising of capital in order to finance growth and expansion. Business organisation began as unincorporated traders and partnerships. By the end of the eighteenth century pressure came to be exerted for the protection of some form of limited liability. This had obvious benefits to owners and investors, perhaps less so for consumers. Limited liability at this point was only available in very specific circumstances and through an Act of Parliament; as a result, few were able to seek this protection. A partnership was essentially the sum of the rights and responsibilities of the individual constituents. A full limited-liability company had a legal personality independent from its shareholders who, in turn, were – largely – independent from the executive leadership of the company. It was the ability to issue and transfer shares freely in the ownership of the company that enabled wider sources and the freer flow of capital. Limited liability did not mean that the capital was not at risk, rather that the risk of the investor was limited to the capital invested, not the total liabilities of the company.

The arrival of limited liability – beginning with the Limited Liability Act of 1856 – was controversial. As Philip Cottrell notes, 'the possible inability of a limited company to meet its debts fully was regarded as immoral.'[26] In addition, freely traded shares could lead to speculation that in turn might lead to a diminution of savings in the economy. Some opponents believed that limited-liability companies opened the way for the domination of large corporate concerns and that the idea of 'limited' invited both the gambler and the fraudulent. However, the essential argument was that of both contractual and trade freedom – that it was in the best interests of both commerce and nation that individuals should be able to contribute to the capital of a business enterprise with their risk limited to that investment and without a full share in the profits and liabilities of the company. Over 20,000 company registrations were formalised in London between 1856 and 1883, although not of all these proceeded to raise capital. Perhaps in the region of 15 per cent of registrations were for private companies – a more limited number of subscribers and shares not freely tradable. All of this shows that, despite the arguments, the benefits of limited liability were taken advantage of as a normal method of business organisation in the period after 1856. Perhaps the reason for this is the increasing dominance of highly capital intensive industry. In the 1850s and 1860s, transport and communications accounted for over half of gross domestic fixed capital formation.[27] It was the necessity of the aggregation of capital to give effect to innovation and commerce to which *The Economist* drew attention in 1926; rather different from its view in 1855 that the importance of limited liability was 'overrated'.[28]

The debate over limited liability is important in its own right in the history of economic development. The dilemmas it posed are amply illustrated in the Quaker businesses.

Christian moral principle was built on personal accountability and responsibility – not least, of course, to God. Those responsibilities included the management of wealth and responsibility for debts incurred. For Quakers, with their heightened sense of responsibility to society, to leave debts owing to others was not only irresponsible but deeply damaging to the reputation of the Society of Friends. As a consequence, bankruptcy was particularly harshly dealt with by the Friends and usually resulted in expulsion by the local meeting. Not all Quakers opposed limited liability: John Bright – the second Quaker MP – supported the proposals. There was perhaps some tension between Quaker moral principle and the Quaker business interest. Bright also opposed a good deal of social and factory reform in the mid nineteenth century. Quaker influence, and indeed lessons for today, are strongest when moral principles, business and a vision for society are combined.

Rowntree converted to a limited-liability company in 1897. The management remained largely within the family, although one external director was appointed. The tragic death of Richard Cadbury in Egypt in 1899 prompted a reorganisation of Cadburys. Transition to a limited-liability company was probably inevitable. The management remained within the family and there were no external shareholders. Joseph Crosfield & Sons had already become a limited company in 1896 – incorporation 'did not involve any surrender of ownership or control by the Crosfields',[29] although again there was one external director.

However, the movement of the Quaker firms into limited joint-stock companies disguised the shifting sands both of succession and indeed of the nature of management.

The internal histories underestimate the impact. The move to limited liability undoubtedly made the raising of loan capital easier; it was simply a matter of time before a wider base of share ownership would be required in order to raise equity. At the same time the hold of the Friends was loosening. The successful entrepreneurial Friends had already largely abandoned the distinctive dress of dark colours and a lack of adornment, designed originally to be an outward demonstration of simplicity of life. Joseph Crosfield's eldest son, George, married a Quaker and remained a Friend for life; his other two sons married out and became Anglicans. The growth of companies also required different approaches to management in order to deal with both scale and diversity as well as increasing departmentalisation and specialisation. The consequence was the growth of professional management. Vision, culture and loyalty did matter; but both family and Quaker influence declined. Tony Corley has noted that only a handful of the 50 wealthy Quaker businessmen he identified between 1860 and 1914 remained within the Society.[30] James Walvin puts it in terms of the third generation of wealth drifting away.[31] By the end of the Second World War, Rowntree had an external chairman and Fry had been absorbed into Cadbury. The latter continued to grow, the merger with Schweppes in 1969 effectively ending the last vestiges of Quaker influence – the enterprise was really no longer under either Quaker or family control, although family members, especially Adrian and Dominic Cadbury, continued to serve the company and the board.

3.2 Responsibilities to employees

We should not underestimate the transformation of the industrial landscape of England in the nineteenth century. Production was mechanised. The capital necessary to achieve this scale meant larger factories and shift working. The demand for labour led to large-scale population shift from the country to the city. The requirement for cheap, nimble and controllable labour meant both unprotected machinery and child labour, with horrific consequences.

Quaker industrialists belonged to a broader tradition of industrial philanthropy,[32] enlightened employers concerned for people and society as well as business. These included Sir Titus Salt and William Lever, as well as the Quakers we have been considering. Essentially the Quaker industrialists represented a form of Christian industrial paternalism that sought to replicate the relationships of either the 'country estate' or the 'family' in the new industrial landscape. Paternalism is too easily dismissed as power and control; in fact it brought many benefits to both employee and employer. However, as a model, rather like the wider Quaker moral influence, it was unable to survive the expansion of ownership and the separation of ownership and control.

The way the Quaker employers related to their employees had two aspects: conditions of employment and moral earnestness. As companies institutionalised and, in some cases, unionised, there was a gradual loss of both moral vision and personal relationships. As a consequence industrial relations became an institutionalised contest of power over terms and conditions.

The family business was run as a family. Joseph Rowntree's rationale for a works magazine was that he was no longer able to keep in personal contact with a workforce that, by 1902, numbered 2,000. Richard Cadbury personally ensured that the female employees of Cadbury were escorted to the station at Bournville. Rowntree established a works library, funded by his own donation together with a compulsory contribution from the workers. However, this rather suggested an unfortunate combination of paternalism and power. Both Cadbury and Rowntree established the classic range of clubs and societies – from friendly societies, savings clubs and clothing clubs to libraries and industrial classes – that characterised the nineteenth-century response to social welfare, combining paternalism with voluntary societies. George Cadbury introduced a sick club to provide for wages for staff who were ill, and an evening sewing class. Savings schemes and clubs were also prevalent at Rowntree. Both of these employers promoted workers outings. Crosfields also had sick clubs and outings.

There is little evidence that the Quaker employers paid better wages per se but certainly, by the beginning of the twentieth century, terms and conditions were formalised and, of course, tinged with Quaker compassion. Rowntree established a pension scheme in 1906, all three of the chocolate magnates provided dental treatment (not so surprising given the industry they were in), half-day and bank holidays were introduced and gradually a more structured approach to wages developed. Crosfields reduced hours – but not wages – in the first decade of the twentieth century and in 1911 introduced new regulations setting out hours, wages, overtime and holidays. There was even a bonus system! Rowntree and Cadbury both made some reductions in the working day and week at around the same time – in the case of Rowntree the formal structure was introduced in 1903. However, the chocolate manufacturers at least relied heavily on casual labour and the Quaker firms had few reservations about the general practice of dismissing women on marriage and young men at age 21 – the younger the cheaper.

These practical aspects of employment were not especially exceptional until combined with the second aspect of 'moral earnestness'. Here the Quaker employers were at their most Christian – and most paternalistic. All the Quaker employers held very dear the spiritual welfare of their workers – and knew what was best for them! Fry, Cadbury and Rowntree all gathered employees for a daily religious service. Joseph Fry was clear that the benefits went wider than the religious:

> …that in addition to the religious benefit that may be looked for, I think there is a great advantage in bringing the workpeople once a day under review. It is often a means of observing their conduct and checking any tendency to impropriety.[33]

Like so many other distinctively Quaker aspects of business, the practice was lost with the growth of the companies and the loss of family control. However, so long as the families controlled the firms, the owners' moral principles were, in varying measures, expounded to, or even imposed upon the workforce.

Edward Cadbury continued to reflect his Quaker principles in the period when he was joint managing director of the firm from 1899 to 1919. He emphasised character and community, was particularly concerned for the welfare of women workers and active in the Anti-Sweating League. In his book *Experiments in Industrial Organization* he emphasised that business efficiency and employee welfare were integrated and that the aim of any industrial organisation is to achieve a spirit of co-operation and goodwill within an ethic of hard work.[34]

Proper perspective is needed. The Quaker businessmen were clear that a well- looked-after and contented labour force was not a luxury but an essential ingredient to business success.[35] The approach secured both loyalty and better returns. The Quakers did stand out as compassionate employers with a genuine concern for their workforces, fed in substantial part by the basic Christian tenets of their belief. They should not be criticised for the paternalism that brought many mutual advantages and the loss of which was not universally beneficial. Ironically it was the combination of paternalism and moralism – perhaps viewed today with even greater disdain than mere paternalism – that shaped their distinctive contribution.

This approach reached its zenith in the model villages.

3.3   The model villages

The Quaker magnates were not the first examples of industrial paternalism, which took a variety of forms, many of a distinctly Tory nature; that is, the employer providing social welfare and other facilities for the employee – compassionate, but within the accepted structures and ordering of society. Industrial paternalism was often an attempt to recreate the forms and structures of traditional rural society in the new industrial landscape. In return for a 'cow and a cottage' or a home and an allotment, deference was offered whether to the squire or the industrialist. Despite the obvious imbalance of power relationships many of the working population welcomed such security.

The idea that industrialists, entrepreneurs and business owners might build 'model villages' is, to many, surprising if not somewhat baffling. These villages remain today as monuments to a bygone age – the era of paternalism and power. The development and existence of the model villages reminds us, however, that in the period of the great Quaker firms, business magnates had a real vision for the relationship of business, family, workforce, locality and wider society. The model villages were an expression of this integrated vision.

The precise social vision varied even if the models were remarkably similar. Indeed the idea of the model village was not exclusively Quaker or even Christian – though they were among the prime examples.

There was always, for some, a quest for perfection. This sometimes took on utopian, even millennial or 'end of the world' overtones. In the midst of William Blake's 'dark, Satanic mills' there must be the building of Jerusalem here on earth. Robert Owen – the early socialist and founder of trade unionism – sought to implement this idea of the perfect community reflecting the expected utopia to come in secular terms. This found expression both in the romanticism of the Lanark mills, the mill and village he acquired in the hills to the south of Glasgow, and on the banks of the River Wabash in Indiana, where the community was even called 'Harmony'. Lanark was an early experiment in social vision around an industrial site. Some model communities were specifically designed to mollify the workers and hence increase production and profitability while maintaining good order – perhaps Port Sunlight in Cheshire, a model village established by William Lever (Lever Brothers) from 1888. A union official described the atmosphere at Port Sunlight as stifling.[36] Model villages had mutual benefits that were generally accepted by those who lived there as well as by those who built the housing stock and planned the landscapes. Vested interest did not just lie with the philanthropic industrialists. The unionisation of workforces did just as much to destroy mutual dependency and familial relationships as the separation of ownership and control in joint-stock companies. The effect of both, however, was effectively to destroy the vision of the business as family – family relationships between individuals were replaced by institutionalised relationships between managers and workers.

The Quakers were responsible for two significant model villages, one in Birmingham and the other in York. The Quaker magnates were also 'ideas people'. The same focused vision and commitment that had led them into industry in the first place gave them both a passion and a compassion for the welfare of those in their charge. These same characteristics and their self-identity as Quakers sometimes made co-operation with others difficult.

The foundation of the Bournville Village Trust in 1900, some 21 years after the Cadbury brothers moved their factory out from the centre of Birmingham, formalised the process of building the Bournville model village. Over 300 hundred houses, almshouses, schools, baths, libraries and the other usual features of the model villages were constructed. The aim was clear: to 'ameliorate the conditions of the labouring classes in Birmingham and elsewhere in Great Britain [by] the provision of improved dwellings'.[37] This was a grand vision, as indeed was that of Joseph Rowntree, who established the more modest model village of New Earswick near York. Quaker idealism was shown in his observation that soup kitchens would never lack for advocates or assistance, 'but an enquiry into the extent and causes of poverty would enlist very little support'.[38]

The realities of the model villages were rather more modest.

Housing was a key aim of the model villages from Bournville to Saltaire, from New Earswick to Port Sunlight. However, it is somewhat misleading to view these villages either as housing for the poor or even simply as housing for the workers. They were aimed more at key – perhaps supervisory – groups of workers for whom housing assistance could contribute significantly to their own aspirations for advancement. Certainly in Bournville the intention was not just the housing of workers at the Cadbury factory. Nevertheless the model adopted was important and instructive, designed to prevent speculators and ensure that the Cadbury vision continued into the future.

The aim of the Quaker promoters was a rent designed to give a commercial return, albeit not profit maximisation. Both Cadbury and Rowntree decided against 'out and out sale at cost price'[39] or anything that had the 'stamp of charity'.[40] The aim was *model* housing, modelling acceptable standards and facilities, with the aim, as Cadbury put it, 'to make it easy for working men to own houses with large gardens'[41] and to enjoy fresh air and light. However, the promoters were conscious of the possibility of speculation if houses could be acquired too cheaply. So the model houses in Bournville were let on 999 year leases, with mortgages offered at 2.5 per cent with a 50 per cent deposit – though with a sliding scale. These ideas were not new and rather than mere paternalism actually reflected a much more aspirational approach to the housing problem. The Quaker social objectives may have been high and intended to assist the poor; in practice it was the respectable working man who was most helped by these schemes. To give a non-Quaker example, the Metropolitan Association for Improving the Dwellings of the Industrious Classes (MAIDIC), formed around 1841, took the view that its aims were most effectively achieved by operating on a proper commercial footing, its shareholders receiving a dividend of up to five per cent per annum. Its memorandum stated:

> That an association be formed for the
> purpose of providing the labouring man with
> an increase of the comforts and conveniences
> of life, with full return to the capitalist.[42]

In 1872 Lord Shaftesbury, a Christian social reformer but also not a Quaker, opened Shaftesbury Park in Battersea, 'a workman's city' for labourers and artisans. This was an estate of 1,200 dwellings built by The Artizans', Labourers' and General Dwellings Company and was a for-profit joint-stock company of which Shaftesbury was President. By 1900 the company had built 6,400 residences in London, accommodating 42,000 people. There were many others, such as the Four Percent Industrial Dwellings Company (the clue being in the name) and the Peabody Trust, as well as various estates developed by Octavia Hill.

There were other examples, and it is perhaps a Quaker weakness that there seemed to be little co-operation on social vision outside of the immediate community.

The model villages themselves tended to represent a rural idyll in the midst of an urban environment. The houses had gardens, there was planned open space (10 per cent of the total acreage), a village green, cricket ground, provision was made for schools, for worship (including a Friends' Meeting House), shops, adult education facilities and so on. There was to be no sale of liquor. The rural vision was clearly in George Cadbury's mind – 'the advantages of outdoor village life, with opportunities for the natural and healthful occupation of cultivating the soil'.[43] The aim was to being spiritual, physical and mental benefit to the occupants.

Criticism ranged from charging rents that were too high to social control. The idyllic atmosphere was, to some at least, suffocating. However, there were not only many mutual benefits – readily appreciated by the inhabitants – but the model villages were a living expression of the wider responsibility of the business community to their localities, the people they employed and the society in which they lived.

4 The responsibility of business to society

The social historian Asa Briggs remarked that many of the Victorian Quaker industrialists 'began by thinking about the family and ended by thinking about society'.[44]

The Quaker vision for society began with their acute sense of the responsibilities of wealth and extended into a wider social vision for society. They were not alone. The history of the Quakers that led to a particular political outlook, together with their tendency to separation, meant that they were unable to co-operate with a good deal of the social reform of the times – mainly because such reform originated in Tory hands. The strength of the Quaker vision was that it was imbued with business responsibility and Christian moral purpose. However, as 'evangelical' influence within the Quakers waned and their cultural identity slowly weakened (numbers declining, less attachment to the dress code and so on), the result was something of a loss of their distinctive moral purpose. This decline simply left a social vision that, however laudable, was increasingly indistinct from either secular or liberal social vision and, at least to an extent, became detached from the original purpose of business.

4.1 The responsibilities of wealth and capital

Prior to the industrial revolution, wealth was generally held in land – the classic landed estates and the county hierarchies of magistrates, squires and Earls. Alongside industrialisation came capital accumulation: financial wealth increasingly held in the hands of the new entrepreneurs – the 'new money' of the period. Similarly concentrations of poverty developed, not least in the new industrial cities of the north as well as, of course, London. The question of responsibility to others and indeed to society exercised many. We have already noted that the Quakers did not generally draw their support from the poorest sections of the community, rather from the artisan and middle classes as well as, increasingly, the entrepreneurs. Quaker families often progressed from a modest prosperity to a significant accumulation of wealth over several generations.

These families faced particular issues of how their faith related to their new-found wealth. George Fox had warned that an excessive preoccupation with riches would dim the Quaker 'inner light'. In 1883 the 'Yearly Meeting' issued 'General Advices' that warned against the snare of wealth accumulation.[45] Quaker quietism seemed unable to cope with the acquisition of wealth, and as we have noted, many drifted away; the impact of evangelical Quakerism was that both the acquisition of wealth and philanthropic responsibility became more open.[46] Indeed, one scholar claims that 'all the prominent Victorian Quaker philanthropists were evangelicals.'[47] Interdenominational societies or committees were the normal evangelical Victorian means of distributing philanthropic funds; classic Quaker quietism was more isolationist than evangelicalism, which by its very nature reached out across denominational lines. Tony Corley quotes a Liverpool businessman, James Cropper (1773–1840), emphasising that riches were held in trust from the Almighty for the good of all humanity.[48] Edward Pease and Joseph Sturge, prominent Quaker businessmen, both worried about the temptations of wealth. Not all Quakers accepted the principles of philanthropy. The Socialist Quaker Society, in the first decade of the twentieth century, criticised business leaders such as George Cadbury, Seebohm Rowntree and Edward Grubb for 'favouring philanthropy to ease social ills rather than more radical steps'.[49] In time the issue became more the accumulation of corporate rather than individual wealth as the joint-stock companies grew.

Quaker businessmen generally both *recognised* and *accepted* the wider responsibilities that came with wealth. However, due to their particular history there was increasing divergence over the way such responsibilities should be expressed.

4.2　A vision for society

The strength of the Quaker business families was that they had a wider vision than simply their business enterprise. This was most fully expressed locally in respect of their workers, factories, towns and cities. Many of the Quaker business leaders also sought to express that social vision more widely. In this they were hampered by their own history and as a result their social vision became closely aligned with a liberal vision that prevented co-operation with some of the major social reforms of the era.

The model villages were one key example of Quaker – and broader – interest in the social welfare of those outside their immediate sphere. Some prominent Quakers certainly went further than that by involvement in their local communities and cities. As early as 1800, Richard Capper Cadbury had served as an Overseer of the Poor as well as on the Board of Street Commissioners for Birmingham. Quakers were very much involved in the anti-slavery movement. John Cadbury, Richard Tapper's son and father of George and Richard, was also an Overseer of the Poor, chairman of the Markets and Fairs Committee and a governor of Birmingham General Hospital. Schooling was also a close interest of the Cadburys, as was, of course, the temperance movement. The imposition of the Cadbury allegiance to the temperance movement onto the Bournville model village is an illustration of the problem of power relationships in paternalism: there was no debate. In 1891 George Cadbury acquired four Birmingham newspapers and later an interest in a national daily; they may not have been a financial success but Cadbury clearly aligned them with the interests of the Liberal Party. He supported Liberal candidates generously and also donated, more modestly, to the Independent Labour Party. Barrow Cadbury (1862-1958), with his wife Geraldine (1865-1941), founded schools and children's homes and a charitable trust. Geraldine was one of the first women magistrates in Birmingham.

The Quakers, with their history of exclusion and persecution by both Church and state, were unlikely to be Tory in politics. Indeed their commitment to Whig toleration, freedom of thought and the idea of progress tended to emphasise that position. In 1833 – a year after the passage of the great Reform Act – Joseph Pease, Quaker businessman, mining and railway magnate, entered Parliament for the newly created South Durham constituency. He sat as a Whig. Outside Parliament Joseph Sturge was engaging in radical activity on the matter of the suffrage and in 1843 another Quaker radical, John Bright, also entered Parliament as a Whig. Bright sat first for Durham, then Manchester and subsequently Birmingham.

Bright was a leading advocate of free trade and prominent in the anti-Corn Law League. As we noted previously, the Corn Laws regulated the price of corn, which in turn maintained the price of bread. The agricultural interest was protected, while the poor paid a high price for a basic staple.

The Tory party had traditionally represented the landed interest. However, with the traditional Tory cries of land, nation and church also came the paternalism we have been discussing. The Tories saw property as giving the right to rule but also the responsibility to care. In 1846 the Tory Prime Minister, Robert Peel, turned Toryism on its head – effectively leading to the foundation of the modern Conservative Party. Peel advocated the repeal of the Corn Laws, thus turning the Tories into a party of free trade.

The implications of this are often misunderstood and are important for appreciating both the impact but also the limitations of Quaker political and social involvement. The Tories became the party of both *social conscience* and *free trade*. The Whigs or Liberals became the party of *political reform* and *free trade*. The consequence was that most of the social legislation of the period came from the Tories, who combined the idea of protective legislation with the voluntary principle for the relief of poverty. Not all Quakers were as passionate as Bright about the pre-eminence of free trade, and certainly from 1870 there was a somewhat wider set of Quaker political allegiances, though only one Quaker entered Parliament as a Conservative during Victoria's reign.

The Earl of Shaftesbury is a case par exemplar.[50] Elected to Parliament as a Tory in 1826, by the time of the Corn

Law crisis he was representing the County of Dorset – largely an agricultural constituency. He changed his mind on the Corn Laws, moving from a protectionist position to one of free trade on the grounds that the poor were best served by cheap bread rather than protection of agricultural incomes. Since he had changed his mind on a matter of principle he resigned his seat, contested the by-election and lost, only to be returned as the MP for Bath 18 months later – still in the Tory interest. Shaftesbury was probably England's premier social reformer. He was responsible for legislation on factory conditions, housing and the prevention of the use of child sweeps. He was also – as an evangelical Christian – committed to the voluntary principle of philanthropy exercised through local societies to those in need. The inability of the Quakers to co-operate in these endeavours is extraordinary; in this instance it was the narrowness of their cultural identity that blinded them to the wider vision.

> The philanthropic protestations of . . . the Quakers . . . have always seemed to have a hollow ring in the light of their hostility or indifference to Shaftesbury's attempts to limit the working-hours of factory children.[51]

One Quaker industrialist, Edmund Ashworth, admitted to employing under-age children. Pease and Bright both opposed Shaftesbury's legislation in Parliament – Shaftesbury describing Bright as his most malignant opponent.

> No Quaker played a prominent part in the
> agitation for the limitation of factory hours.
> Where they appear in its history at all, it is
> almost always as its inveterate opponents.[52]

The antipathy of the Quakers towards the Tories
prevented co-operation on matters of national importance
and emphasised that Quaker activism was at its most
powerful in the local sphere. The Quaker magnates
excelled in their own empires, rather like the old Tory
squires. Their vision and social concern was genuine; their
isolationism and history of exclusion meant that their
involvement on the wider, national political scene was
often determined by narrow political concerns rather than
the broad social vision they were so committed to locally.

5   Lessons for today

The Quaker businesses were extraordinary companies led by outstanding examples of leadership. In their historical context the story brings to light many characteristics and influences that help explain their distinctiveness. We have seen how these Quaker industrialists harnessed all of their intellectual and personal prowess to create wealth, develop technology, grow companies and harness capital. Yet due in part to their own history of persecution but also to the depth of their spiritual beliefs, the Quakers sought to develop business practices and models that reflected a moral passion for honesty and integrity, not least in respect of relationships and care for employees. Alongside this they had a vision, especially for the local community, though perhaps less successfully more widely, which located business and wealth in a wider context.

The Quakers cannot simply be copied or replicated today in a very different economic and social context. However, there are a good number of principles that can indeed be used to reflect very deeply today upon business practice; the experience of the last several years does at least suggest that we have a great deal to learn.

1   *Wealth creation as a moral responsibility*

Business today needs to articulate its moral purpose. This is not intended to mean that business should preach some form of behavioural moralism, rather that it needs to be clear about purpose, the good that business contributes to society, the encouragement of innovation and growth and the moral responsibility of creating wealth.

One consequence of the way business has become detached from its moral purpose is the loss of a real understanding of the role and place of wealth creation.

Business has a moral responsibility to create wealth – which is not simply about profit. The Quaker businesses understood this imperative and harnessed their passion and creativity to economic development and growth. The Quaker businesses also pursued quality alongside trust and confidence. They did so, not simply to follow the rules of a moral code, but because to do so also made excellent business sense. So this raises the question of the relationship of moral purpose, business objectives and the maximisation of shareholder value.

The moral imperative to create wealth carries a responsibility that goes beyond the maximisation of profit or shareholder value. This wider purpose extends further than moral codes, regulation, business ethics and social responsibility. Perhaps this can be summed up in two words, *stewardship* and *reputation*. The real moral purpose of the business, exemplified by the Quakers, is to steward the purposes, objectives and capital of the original founders in the creation of wealth and value for all stakeholders. To do so will enhance the reputation of a company for quality, employee relations, the supply chain, environmental sustainability and social value. This lay at the heart of the Quaker vision.

2   The centrality of culture and networks in forming entrepreneurs

Entrepreneurs do not flourish alone. In some ways that might seem somewhat strange because rugged individualism, risk-taking and even a degree of eccentricity mark out the entrepreneur. However, what the Quakers have shown is the way culture shapes the businesses and the entrepreneurial leaders. The powerful strength of networks that the Quakers developed fundamentally formed and shaped the business environment and culture of trust and confidence that is essential for any successful entrepreneur or business leader. Culture shapes organisations and leadership is central in forming culture. Antony Jenkins, the Group Chief Executive of Barclays Bank, illustrates the importance of culture in his comment that 'for our Values to have true meaning, employees need to live and breathe them.'[53] It is the culture of an organisation which allows this 'living and breathing.' What the Quakers amply demonstrated was that values, culture and behaviour are intricately linked and cannot be separated.

3   A discipline that shaped character

Spiritual discipline played a crucial part in shaping the character of the Quakers in business. This character was formed through the intensity and identity of the family, the Quaker Meeting, schools and businesses. As a consequence, important characteristics came to the fore: integrity, trust, honesty, patience, creativity, determination and responsibility. These are the essential ingredients of entrepreneurial character. In addition to that, an inquisitive mind, an appreciation of stewardship and an outlook that recognises the wider responsibilities of business all contribute to a sense of vision and purpose. This character encouraged entrepreneurial risk-taking – new industries, new technologies – while the Quaker business leaders still remained conservative on matters that seemed to challenge their moral code, such as advertising. The instilling of discipline, even moral discipline, seems neglected today in modern business education and preparation. The acceptance of responsibility for actions lay at the heart of the character formed by Quaker discipline. In a sense this was the dilemma posed by limited liability. The restriction of potential losses to the amount of the investment encouraged entrepreneurial risk-taking; but without personal responsibility for actions and behaviour in the market, carried its own risk of encouraging not investment but irresponsible behaviour. We would do well to talk about this dilemma more in contemporary debate.

4   *A faith that formed a clear moral code*

Perhaps the most difficult thing to reflect upon in drawing lessons for today is morality and a moral code of behaviour. Modern society values its diversity and freedom. Many would balk at anything that suggested a code of moral behaviour, other than in the broadest terms. Religion, which historically has been the main provider of such moral frameworks, is largely marginalised, in the business world at least.

Many companies have business principles or statements of values that adorn the walls of the board room or the annual report. Corporate social responsibility reports have become longer and more intense, and companies often involve themselves in charitable endeavours. Welcome though this may be, it is impossible to separate personal moral behaviour from business culture and behaviour in the market place.

Professionalism cannot be entirely separated from morality, not least in the light of the experience of the traumas in the financial services sector and the consequences across the economy.

The Quakers certainly understood that their spiritual beliefs formed a moral code of behaviour. Some form of acceptance of moral norms, basic principles and professionalism should surely inform all business leadership today. The advent of licensing for bankers may indeed be an appropriate response to the ethical issues which have emerged in the financial services sector. However, a regulatory approach will not succeed without personal commitment, professional and indeed, personal ethical responsibility and behaviour.

5   *A passion for education and training*

The exclusion of the Quakers from universities in particular not only caused many to apply their intellectual endeavours to business but gave them a passion for education and training. The experience of exclusion and the strength of the Quaker network in shaping culture and identity both contributed to the importance given to apprenticeships and business education.

However, the vision for education went further, through the establishment of their own schools. While this was clearly intended at least in part to preserve Quaker identity, the recognition of the centrality of education for both business and life is instructive. The Quaker school shaped a Quaker culture; the Quaker apprenticeship moulded a business culture. Education was not just schooling; it was part of life.

Business and education belong together for training not only in business skills but also for the formation of character, personality and life skills that shape the very nature of leadership in business and society. The lesson from the Quakers is the central importance of the inquisitive and creative mind and the harnessing of these characteristics and skills in the business enterprise.

6   The centrality of the privately owned family business model

The family was central to the Quaker business leaders because they viewed their businesses as extensions of the family. This had profound implications for the way their businesses were managed and grew and, indeed, for the relationship with both employees and local communities.

The unique value of the family business is that it provides a setting where culture and character can work together in the stewardship of values, succession and patient entrepreneurship.

The family firm as a business organisation did, however, face many challenges with the arrival of limited-liability and joint-stock companies. British family firms tended to develop in different ways from their European counterparts, family ownership rarely lasting more than a couple of generations, especially with growth by acquisition and merger. Ownership was rapidly dispersed. This was in stark contrast to the long-term family ownership of European family businesses. We have lessons to learn about commitment, governance and indeed structure.

In today's complex business world we need new means of encouraging family businesses but also fresh and creative approaches to wider questions of share ownership and structure. The debates over the moral dilemmas of limited liability does not mean that the classic form of business structure today for raising capital and managing growth can or should be abandoned. However, it does act as a reminder that family businesses and other alternative forms and structures of ownership may have a significant role to play in the moral economy of the future. Incentives for entrepreneurs, the self-employed and family businesses may have a part to play; but financial and tax incentives will not be effective apart from the wider issues of business culture, character development and moral behaviour. As well as family businesses, other forms of ownership, including mutual structures, private equity and new classes of equity shares, may all have a role in reassessing ownership and control.

7   *Understanding employee relations*

The Quakers were not perfect and they were not perfect employers. They did not necessarily pay above the market rate and were as concerned to ensure good value in labour as in anything else. They were certainly at the forefront of many developments in employee practices, even if they were not the pioneers.

However, in two respects there are important lessons for us from the Quakers in the area of employee relationships.

First, the Quakers understood the fundamental premise that the efficiency of the business and the welfare of the employees were not only intricately related but positively correlated. This did not mean that high standards were not demanded, nor did it mean that employees were simply given higher wages or benefits. Rather it was about an attitude of mind, centring on mutual loyalty and interdependence. There was a direct relationship between employers and employees which, in family businesses, was not mediated through intermediate levels of management or unionisation. In addition there was a mutuality in purpose – namely aspiration to produce quality – and an acceptance that the prospects of worker and owner were interrelated.

Second, the Quakers had a holistic view of their responsibilities to employees. The model village concept may not be repeatable today but it was a practical concept that conveyed an understanding of the responsibility of employers for the health, housing and educational welfare of those in their charge. Perhaps today that responsibility is a shared one (whether in health or pension provision); perhaps also it could go further.

8   A vision for business in society, especially the local

Business has, in too many respects, become compartmentalised in society, so that people cannot see the links between business, wealth, responsibility and society. This is a moral question. You cannot behave amorally in one sector of life and then seek to 'do good' in another without disastrous consequences.[54]

The Quaker business leaders remind us of the importance of these links, especially in the locality where business is located. Perhaps one of the complexities of globalisation in business is a lack of material location, with a consequential lack of sense of any local responsibility.

Business responsibility to society is not about corporate social responsibility as such. Rather it is primarily about recognising responsibility to the wider society in which the business is set, especially in local communities. It is essentially about integration. Education, partnerships with other businesses, employee participation and community involvement might all feature.

In this paper we have not sought to make formal policy proposals. However, to give an example of how to encourage small, local businesses or entrepreneurs in their local responsibilities: if a company gives a person's time to a community or education project (school governor, training), then allocating a value to that time and allowing the company to claim this as an allowance against corporation tax and the individual against income tax might transform business and personal involvement in the community.

9   Understanding the responsibilities of wealth and capital

The worst examples of excess in the last decade have helped no one, damaged business's reputation and increased the sense of disconnect many feel from wider society.

The Quaker business leaders remind us that the acquisition of wealth and capital carries responsibilities. Those responsibilities include the imperative of investment, saving, encouraging employees, community involvement and charitable giving. In essence, despite probable resistance today to the terminology, this could be seen to represent 'a moral community.'

Many business leaders today of course practise those virtues, though not all. We would do well if they were inculcated in business schools, training and in character development, so that when we come to exercise such responsibilities it is not because we think we have to but because we desire to.

10   Applying commercial solutions to social problems

The Quaker businesses remind us that vision, character, wealth, responsibility and a concern for society do not need to be separated from a wealth-creating, efficient business enterprise. Indeed in the model villages and in many of the provisions for social welfare with which they were associated, the Quaker leaders demonstrated that the application of commercial principles – which differs from profit maximization; though certain involves profit satisfaction, and perhaps the maximisation of shared rather than simply shareholder value – was often the best way to ensure the most effective social support for those in need. In this way aspiration, self-help, independence and appropriate charitable assistance could often be harnessed to greatest effect.

Whether an individual should become a Quaker, an evangelical Christian or any other form of religious adherence is of course a matter for individuals beyond the scope of this paper. However, whatever our religious or other affiliation, perhaps we might all be permitted to say:

> Thank God for the Quakers, their business leadership and the lessons they teach us today.

Bibliography

Ackrill, M. and Hannah, L., *Barclays: the Business of Banking, 1690–1996*, Cambridge: CUP, 2001.

Briggs, A., *Seebohm Rowntree, 1871–1954*, London: Longmans, 1961.

Cadbury, D., *Chocolate Wars: From Cadbury to Kraft – 200 Years of Sweet Success and Bitter Rivalry*, London: HarperPress, 2010.

Church, R. A., *The Great Victorian Boom 1850–1873*, London: Macmillan, 1975.

Church, R. A., 'Problems and Perspectives', in R. A. Church (ed.), *The Dynamics of Victorian Business: Problems and Perspectives to the 1870*, London: Allen & Unwin, 1980.

Corley, T. A. B., 'Changing Quaker Attitudes to Wealth, 1690–1950', in D. J. Jeremy (ed.), *Religion, Business and Wealth in Modern Britain*, London and New York: Routledge, 1998.

Corley, T. A. B., 'How Quakers Coped with Business Success: Quaker Industrialists 1860–1914', in D. J. Jeremy (ed.), *Business and Religion in Britain*, Aldershot: Gower Press, 1987.

Cottrell, P. L., *Industrial Finance 1830–1914: The Finance and Organization of English Manufacturing Industry*, London and New York: Methuen, 1980.

Donnachie, I. and Hewitt, G., *Historic New Lanark: The Dale and Owen Industrial Community since 1785*, Edinburgh: Edinburgh University Press, 1993.

Henslowe, P., *Ninety Years On: An Account of the Bournville Village Trust*, Birmingham: Bournville Village Trust, 1984.

Hunt, B. C., *The Development of the Business Corporation in England 1800–1867*, Cambridge, MA: Harvard University Press, 1936.

Isichei, E. A., *Victorian Quakers*, London: Oxford University Press, 1970.

Joseph Rowntree Village Trust, *One Man's Vision: The Story of the Joseph Rowntree Village Trust*, London: Allen & Unwin, 1954.

Kimberley, J., 'Edward Cadbury: A Neglected Management Thinker?', in *The Friends Quarterly*, issue 4, 2013.

Kirby, M. W., *The Origins of Railway Enterprise: The Stockton and Darlington Railway, 1821–1863*, Cambridge: Cambridge University Press, 1993.

Mayer, C. P., *Firm Commitment: Why the Corporation is Failing us and How to Restore Trust in it*, Oxford: Oxford University Press, 2013.

Musson, A. E., *Enterprise in Soap and Chemicals: Joseph Crosfield & Sons, Limited, 1815–1965*, Manchester: Manchester University Press, 1965.

Pollard, C.W., *The Tides of Life*, Wheaton, Crossway, 2014

Prior, A. and Kirby, M. W., 'The Society of Friends and Business Culture 1700–1830', in D. J. Jeremy (ed.), *Religion, Business and Wealth in Modern Britain*, London and New York: Routledge, 1998.

Punshon, J., *Portrait in Grey: A Story History of the Quakers*, London: Quaker Home Service, 1984; revised and reprinted 1986, 1991.

Raistrick, A., *Quakers in Science and Industry: Being an Account of the Quaker Contributions to Science and Industry during the 17th and 18th Centuries*, York: Sessions Book Trust, 1950; reprinted 1993.

Sutton, G. B., *A History of Shoemaking in Street, Somerset: C. & J. Clark, 1833–1903*, York: William Sessions, 1979.

Tregoning, D. and Cockerell, H. A. L., *Friends for Life: Friends' Provident Life Office 1832–1982*, London: Henry Melland, 1982.

Turnbull, R. D., *Shaftesbury: The Great Reformer*, Oxford: Lion Hudson, 2010.

Wagner, G., *The Chocolate Conscience*, London: Chatto & Windus, 1987.

Walvin, J., *The Quakers: Money and Morals*, London: John Murray, 1997.

Notes

[1] P. L. Cottrell, *Industrial Finance 1830–1914: The Finance and Organization of English Manufacturing Industry*, London and New York: Methuen, 1980, pp. 3, 5.

[2] A. Raistrick, *Quakers in Science and Industry: Being an Account of the Quaker Contributions to Science and Industry during the 17th and 18th Centuries*, York: Sessions Book Trust, 1950; reprinted 1993, p. 89.

[3] J. Punshon, *Portrait in Grey: A Story History of the Quakers*, London: Quaker Home Service, 1984; revised and reprinted 1986, 1991, p. 50.

[4] J. Walvin, *The Quakers: Money and Morals*, London: John Murray, 1997, ch. 2.

[5] A. Prior and M. Kirby, 'The Society of Friends and Business Culture 1700–1830', in D. J. Jeremy (ed.), *Religion, Business and Wealth in Modern Britain*, London and New York: Routledge, 1998, pp. 115–36.

[6] Prior and Kirby, 'Society of Friends', p. 115.

[7] Prior and Kirby, 'Society of Friends', p. 116.

[8] Raistrick, *Quakers in Science and Industry*, p. 29.

[9] Raistrick, *Quakers in Science and Industry*, p. 43.

[10] Walvin, *The Quakers*, p. 98.

[11] D. Tregoning and H. Cockerell, *Friends for Life: Friends' Provident Life Office 1832–1982*, London: Henry Melland, 1982, p. 16.

[12] C. Mayer, *Firm Commitment: Why the Corporation is Failing us and How to Restore Trust In it*, Oxford: Oxford University Press, 2013, p. 239.

[13] E. Isichei, *Victorian Quakers*, London: Oxford University Press, 1970, p. 183.

[14] For practical purposes an evangelical is a Christian who understands the Bible to be the ultimate authoritative source of faith and doctrine. For a more detail description see R.D. Turnbull, *Anglican and Evangelical?* London: Bloomsbury, 2007

[15] Isichei, *Victorian Quakers*, p. 7.

[16] Raistrick, *Quakers in Science and Industry*, p. 46.

[17] Raistrick, *Quakers in Science and Industry*, p. 48.

[18] Walvin, *The Quakers*, p. 82.

[19] Isichei, *Victorian Quakers*, p. 185.

[20] G. B. Sutton, *A History of Shoemaking in Street, Somerset: C. & J. Clark*, York: William Sessions, 1979, pp. 200–1.

[21] M. Ackrill and L. Hannah, *Barclays: The Business of Banking, 1690–1996*, Cambridge: CUP, 2001, pp. 24, 32.

[22] Ackrill and Hannah, *Barclays*, p. 37.

[23] Ackrill and Hannah, *Barclays*, p. 38.

[24] M. W. Kirby, *The Origins of Railway Enterprise: The Stockton and Darlington Railway, 1821–1863*, Cambridge: Cambridge University Press, 1993, p. 79.

[25] R. A. Church, 'Problems and Perspectives', in R. A. Church (ed.), *The Dynamics of Victorian Business: Problems and Perspectives to the 1870*, London: Allen & Unwin, 1980, p. 19.

[26] Cottrell, *Industrial Finance*, p. 41.

[27] Church, 'Problems and perspectives', pp. 26–7.

[28] Quoted in B. C. Hunt, *The Development of the Business Corporation in England 1800–1867*, Cambridge, MA: Harvard University Press, 1936, p. 116.

[29] A. E. Musson, *Enterprise in Soap and Chemicals: Joseph Crosfield & Sons, Limited, 1815–1965*, Manchester: Manchester University Press, 1965, p. 139.

[30] T. A. B. Corley 'How Quakers Coped with Business Success: Quaker Industrialists 1860–1914', in D. J. Jeremy (ed.), *Business and Religion in Britain*, Aldershot: Gower Press, 1987.

[31] Walvin, *The Quakers*, p. 193.

[32] Walvin, *The Quakers*, p. 179.

[33] G. Wagner, *The Chocolate Conscience*, London: Chatto & Windus, 1987, p. 51.

[34] J. Kimberley, 'Edward Cadbury: A Neglected Management Thinker?', in *The Friends Quarterly*, issue 4, 2013.

[35] Walvin, *The Quakers*, pp. 184, 187.

[36] Wagner, *Chocolate Conscience*, p. 71.

[37] P. Henslowe, *Ninety Years On: An Account of the Bournville Village Trust*, Birmingham: Bournville Village Trust, 1984.

[38] Joseph Rowntree Village Trust, *One Man's Vision: The Story of the Joseph Rowntree Village Trust*, London: Allen & Unwin, 1954, p. 5.

[39] Henslowe, *Ninety Years On*, p. 3.

[40] Joseph Rowntree Village Trust, *One Man's Vision*, p. 4.

[41] Henslowe, *Ninety Years On*, p. 3.

[42] Metropolitan Association for Improving the Dwellings of the Industrious Classes, 1841.

[43] Walvin, *The Quakers*, p. 189.

[44] A. Briggs, *Seebohm Rowntree, 1871–1954*, London: Longmans, 1961, p. 7.

[45] T. A. B. Corley, 'Changing Quaker Attitudes to Wealth, 1690–1950', in D. J. Jeremy (ed.), *Religion, Business and Wealth in Modern Britain*, London and New York: Routledge, 1998.

[46] Walvin, *The Quakers*, pp. 128–9 ; Punshon, *Portrait in Grey*, pp. 166–7.

[47] Isichei, *Victorian Quakers*, p. 214.

[48] Corley, 'Changing Quaker Attitudes to Wealth.

[49] Corley, 'Changing Quaker Attitudes to Wealth.

[50] R. D. Turnbull, *Shaftesbury: The Great Reformer*, Oxford: Lion Hudson, 2010.

[51] Isichei, *Victorian Quakers*, p. 246.

[52] Isichei, *Victorian Quakers*, p. 247.

[53] Antony Jenkins, Barclays Bank, http://www.barclays.com/about-barclays/barclays-values.html

[54] C.W. Pollard, *The Tides of Life*, Crossway, page 154-155